SCIENCE
FUNDAMENTALS

THE SCIENCE OF
ENERGY

AUTHOR:

MASON CREST

MASON CREST

MASON CREST
450 Parkway Drive, Suite D
Broomall, PA 19008
(866) MCP-BOOK (toll free)
www.masoncrest.com

First printing
1 3 5 7 9 8 6 4 2

Library of Congress Cataloging-in-Publication Data

The science of energy.
  pages cm. — (Science fundamentals)
Audience: Age 14.
Audience: Grades 7 to 8.
Includes bibliographical references and index.
ISBN 978-1-4222-3513-3 (hc) — ISBN 978-1-4222-8333-2 (ebook)
1. Force and energy—Juvenile literature. 2. Dynamics—Juvenile literature. 3. Physics—Juvenile literature.
QC73.4.S35 2017
531.6—dc23
2015035337

Science Fundamentals Series ISBN: 978-1-4222-3512-6

SCIENCE FUNDAMENTALS

THE SCIENCE OF ENERGY
THE SCIENCE OF LIFE
THE SCIENCE OF SPACE
THE SCIENCE OF TIME

PICTURE CREDITS

Page:
5: Pat Corkery, United Launch Alliance, 6, 8, 10, 12, 14, 16, 18, 22, 32, 33, 34, 38, 44: Used under license from Shutterstock, Inc.; 9, 13, 17, 18, 23, 24, 25, 28, 29, 33, 34, 35: Wellcome Library, London; 18: Everett Historical; 30: Wikimedia Commons; 39, 42: Library of Congress; 41: NASA/SDO; 43: U.S. Department of Energy

Vector Illustrations: 7,11,15,21,27,31,36,40,45: rzarek/Shutterstock.com

Background Images: 2, 13, 30: Hyena Reality/Shutterstock.com; 8, 14, 20, 26, 28, 34, 38, 40: Digital_Art/Shutterstock.com; 10, 16: BackgroundStore/Shutterstock.com; 16: vlastas/Shutterstock.com; 24: TairA/Shutterstock.com

Table of Contents

KEY ICONS TO LOOK FOR:

Words to Understand: These words with their easy-to-understand definitions will increase the reader's understanding of the text, while building vocabulary skills.

Sidebars: This boxed material within the main text allows readers to build knowledge, gain insights, explore possibilities, and broaden their perspectives by weaving together additional information to provide realistic and holistic perspectives.

Research Projects: Readers are pointed toward areas of further inquiry connected to each chapter. Suggestions are provided for projects that encourage deeper research and analysis.

Text-Dependent Questions: These questions send the reader back to the text for more careful attention to the evidence presented there.

Series Glossary of Key Terms: This back-of-the book glossary contains terminology used throughout this series. Words found here increase the reader's ability to read and comprehend higher-level books and articles in this field.

Chapter 1

MAKING IT WORK

The search for an understanding of energy, the stuff that drives the Universe, has fascinated people for centuries.

Have you ever felt full of energy? When you do you feel that you can make all sorts of things happen. You can **work** hard if you want to, or you can play for hours. If this is what you mean by energy then you are very close to what a scientist means by it. The word itself comes from the Greek word *energeia*, which means "in work." Energy can make things happen. Energy makes things warmer, energy can move things, energy can make things brighter and energy can help living things grow.

The more energy there is the more it can do, just as you can do more when you have lots of energy. If a scientist describes an object as "energetic," he or she means that the object can do things. For instance, if you see a ball on the ground it should be pretty obvious that it doesn't have much energy. It isn't doing anything just lying there. However, if you give it some energy by kicking it, it will be able to do things, such as breaking a window if you're careless about the direction you kick it in! The ball didn't suddenly get its energy from nowhere. You had to give it the energy it needed to leave the ground and move through the air.

DIFFERENT FORMS OF ENERGY

As we shall see, scientists believe that the amount of energy in the Universe always stays the same. It is impossible to make new energy. This means that if you want to make something happen you have to transfer energy from somewhere else. When you kick a ball, you use **chemical energy** in your muscles to move your leg and give the ball **movement energy**. The chemical energy in your muscles comes from chemical energy in your food.

An enormous amount of energy is required to fire a rocket into orbit around the Earth. During the launch, the chemical energy stored in the rocket's fuel is converted in a controlled way into the movement energy needed for lift-off.

When you play a sport such as basketball, food energy stored in your muscles is constantly being converted into the movement energy you need to run and to throw the ball. You pass some of that energy on to the ball when you shoot, while some of the energy is lost from your body as heat.

Energy comes in different forms and can be switched from one form to another. Two forms have been mentioned already, chemical energy—part of what is called **internal energy**—stored in substances, and movement energy. How many more can you think of? Light, sound, heat and electricity are all forms of energy. The string of a bow pulled tight is storing energy, called **potential energy**, which is converted to movement energy in the arrow when the string is released.

The peoples of the ancient world didn't think in terms of abstract ideas like energy when they thought about the way the world worked. They used gods and other mythical beings to explain why things behave as they do. The word *energy*, in the sense we understand it now, was first used in the 1840s by William Thomson. We will be meeting him later in the story. However, the early Greek philosophers had some interesting ideas and we turn to them first to begin our exploration of energy.

When the archer pulls back the bowstring chemical energy stored in the archer's arm muscles is converted into potential energy in the stretched string. When the archer lets go of the string the potential energy is suddenly changed into movement energy, which is passed on to the arrow, making it fly towards the target.

WORDS TO UNDERSTAND

chemical energy—energy stored in the links that hold atoms together when they join to form groups of atoms, called molecules.

internal energy—the total heat energy and chemical energy within an object.

movement energy—the energy an object has in motion. Also called kinetic energy.

potential energy—energy stored in an object, such as the energy stored in a coiled spring which is released as kinetic energy when the spring unwinds.

work—a measure of the energy transferred to or from an object or a system. Work involves the action of a force on the object or system and is measured in joules.

RESEARCH PROJECT

The famed physicist Richard Feynman, sometimes known as the "great explainer," discusses the nature of energy and light waves in a short video, available at https://www.youtube.com/watch?v=FjHJ7FmVOM4.

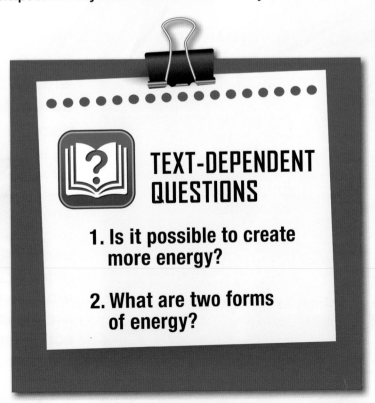

TEXT-DEPENDENT QUESTIONS

1. Is it possible to create more energy?

2. What are two forms of energy?

Chapter 2
COSMIC MIND

Our scientific understanding of matter and of how energy can change it owes much to the theories of ancient Greek thinkers.

Anaxagoras (c.500–428 BCE) was one of the first people we know about who thought seriously about the nature of the Universe and the way it worked. He wanted to explain why matter behaves as it does, for example why it moves and changes in certain ways. He wasn't satisfied with the explanation that was usually given at the time, which was that matter behaves as it does because it is in its nature to do so. Anaxagoras was looking for something—some sort of **force**—that would link the seemingly infinite variety of matter and all the changes and interactions that could possibly be produced in it. Whatever this link or guiding force was, Anaxagoras was certain of one thing. It must have no mythical character or have anything to do with gods. It had to be absolutely logical and rational and be able to account for everything he saw in the Universe. Anaxagoras gave his force the name **nous**, which means "mind" or "reason."He believed that the Universe came into being through the action of *nous* on an infinite number of "seeds."

The huge amount of energy released during a lightning flash can join together particles of different chemicals in the air to produce new ones. This is rather like the idea of a cosmic force acting on "seeds," proposed by the Greek scientist Anaxagoras.

This Medieval manuscript illustration represents three of the greatest
ancient Greek scientists: Plato, Anaxagoras, and Democritus.
Anaxagoras believed that the Universe came about through the action
of a cosmic mind, or *nous*, on an infinite number of particles, or
"seeds." Democritus was the first person to say that matter consisted
of particles that could not be divided into smaller parts. He called these
particles *atoms*.

THE COSMIC MIND AT WORK

Anaxagoras's seeds were similar to what we would think of today as atoms.
The idea that everything was made up of tiny particles too small to see had
been put forward by another Greek, Leucippus, who lived around the same
time as Anaxagoras. Our word "atom" comes from the Greek *atomein*, which
means "cannot be divided." Anaxagoras's seeds, however, could be divided an
infinite number of times. The idea that atoms could not be divided came from
Leucippus's pupil Democritus (470–380 BCE).

All the order and forms around us came into being, Anaxagoras believed, by
the action of *nous*, the cosmic mind, shaping the substance of the Universe.
"Mind rules the world and has brought order out of confusion," he said. If
Anaxagoras's seeds can be seen as atoms then perhaps we might also think
of his *nous* as being like energy. It was the force that moved the Universe and
determined its shape.

This has some similarity to our current ideas about the origin of the Universe. Most scientists now believe that it started with a colossal explosion of energy, which has been called the **big bang**. For a while the Universe was pure energy, but after a time particles of matter formed out of it. These particles came together to produce all the matter in the Universe today. If you substitute *nous* for "energy" and *seeds* for "particles of matter" in those sentences, it sounds very similar to Anaxagoras's idea, doesn't it?

Anaxagoras's ideas were not very popular. In fact, he was put on trial for his beliefs. Later Greek thinkers, such as Aristotle (384–322 BCE), had a greater influence. He founded the Lyceum, a school of study in Athens, around 335 BCE. Aristotle put the emphasis on collecting information and on sorting and classifying everything. Yet Aristotle did not believe in experiment, only in observation. He called his study physics. He believed that things had certain "causes." The aim of Aristotle's **physics** was to discover the nature of things. Everything had a "final cause," which was the object's purpose for existence. Because everything was seen as having a purpose the Universe came to be viewed as rather like a living thing. There was no point in looking for the force or energy that moved things; they were simply fulfilling their purpose. Aristotle did try to put together laws that would explain why things moved, but these simply came down to saying that, for example, objects fall because that is the natural thing for them to do. He never tried to back up his ideas by experiment. Aristotle's view of the world dominated thinking for the next thousand years.

Aristotle believed that everything had a purpose, or "final cause," and that an object would behave according to its purpose. He did not attempt to test his ideas by experiment, however.

WORDS TO UNDERSTAND

big bang—the name given to the theory that all the matter and energy in the Universe originated in a sudden explosion outwards from a single point, about 15 billion years ago.

force—a power or agency that affects the movement or behavior of an object.

nous—the name the Greek philosopher Anaxagoras gave to the force he believed guided and ordered the behavior of the Universe.

physics—the study of the laws, or rules, that determine the behavior of the matter and energy in the Universe.

RESEARCH PROJECT

Using the Internet or your school library, do some research on one of the following ancient Greek scientists: Anaxagoras, Leucippus, Democritus, Plato, or Aristotle. Write a two-page report on this person's accomplishments, and present it to your class.

## TEXT-DEPENDENT QUESTIONS

1. What name did Anaxagoras give to the force that he believed would cause matter to move and change in certain ways?

2. What was the aim of Aristotle's science of physics?

Chapter 3

LIVING ENERGY

Seventeenth-century scientists performed experiments that gave a better understanding of the energy changes that take place when an object moves.

The first real experiments into the behavior of moving objects were conducted by Galileo Galilei (1564–1642), the Italian astronomer and physicist. Although Galileo could not have understood energy as we understand it today, he seems to have had an awareness that the energy of an object thrown vertically upwards, a ball say, does not gradually disappear as it reaches the top of its flight. The energy is, in fact, changing from one form into another, from energy of movement into energy of position. We now call these ideas **kinetic energy** and potential energy. As the object reaches its highest point all of its kinetic energy has become potential energy and for a split second the ball stops moving. As it starts to fall, the ball's potential energy is changed back again into kinetic energy so that when it reaches the ground it has just as much kinetic energy as it had when it was first thrown up.

A ball is given kinetic energy when it is thrown into the air. At its highest point it has no kinetic energy, but it has maximum potential energy.

Aristotle had said that in order to keep moving a body had to have a force applied to it continuously. This was supposedly provided by air rushing in to fill the space left by the moving object. Later, others pointed out that if this was true then moving objects should travel faster and faster. Galileo showed that this point of view was the correct one. He measured the velocities of objects moving on slopes, on level surfaces and falling freely. He showed that an object moving down a slope or falling freely accelerates, that is, its velocity increases, but on a flat surface its **velocity** stays the same. The increase in velocity of a falling object is caused by the constant pull of the Earth.

VELOCITY AND MOMENTUM

Every moving object has a quality called **momentum**. This is found by multiplying the **mass** of the object, which is the amount of material it contains, by its velocity (written as v). the more massive an object is and the faster it is travelling, the more momentum it will have. How does the object gain momentum? To get something moving you have to apply a force to it, perhaps by pushing it or firing it from a gun. Whatever you do you are turning one form of energy into movement energy.

Galileo was the first scientist to measure the velocities of moving objects. He determined that a ball will remain stationary until a force acts upon it to move it.

The amount of energy a moving object has can be worked out from the force needed to get it moving at a certain velocity. If we do this we find that the amount of energy in a moving object is equal to a half times its mass (written as m), multiplied by its velocity squared, a definition first given by the Frenchman Gaspard de Coriolis (1792–1843). This fundamental law can be written simply as: kinetic energy = $1/2 \ mv^2$.

Galileo's work on moving objects was continued by Christian Huygens (1629–1795), a Dutch scientist. Huygens showed that the momentum of moving objects is always conserved. That is to say, it cannot be created or destroyed, only exchanged between different objects. If two objects collide head on, one with a momentum of x, say, and the other with a momentum of y, then the total momentum at the time of the collision is x plus y. Measuring the speed and direction of the objects after the collision shows that the total momentum is still x plus y. This was the first step along the path to showing that energy was conserved, a principle that would be demonstrated by Hermann Helmholtz 150 years later.

VIS VIVA—THE LIVING FORCE

In 1686 the German mathematician Gottfried Leibniz (1646–1716) introduced the Latin term *vis viva*, which means living force. This concept was very similar to the idea of kinetic energy worked out much later, in the nineteenth century, in that the **vis viva** of an object depended on both its mass and on its velocity. Several scientists, including the Dutchman Willem s'Gravesande (1688–1742) and the Marquise du Châtelet, Gabrielle de Breteuil (c.1700–1749), were impressed by Leibniz's idea and carried out experiments to test it.

S'Gravesande built a variety of machines to experiment with motion, such as one in which a moving metal ball on a thread was made to strike a stationary similar ball. By knowing the masses of the balls and their velocities before and after the collision, s'Gravesande could calculate how much *vis viva* was in each ball. It seemed that the *vis viva* could be transferred almost entirely from the moving ball to the stationary one.

One of the most famous English scientists, Isaac Newton (1642–1727), made many contributions to the study of energy and forces. Among Newton's greatest contributions were his **laws of motion**, describing the way objects move. In doing so he built on work done by Galileo over a hundred years earlier. The science of moving objects was brought to a peak by Newton, whose laws could be used to explain everything from an arrow travelling towards its target to the motion of the Moon around the Earth.

An object accelerates rapidly when it is free to fall. Galileo found that, whatever the mass of the object, it always accelerates at the same rate.

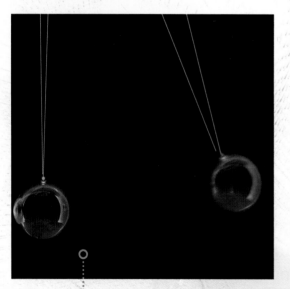

S'Gravesande investigated the amount of *vis viva* that could be passed on when one ball collided with another.

RESEARCH PROJECT

Find out about a device known as "Newton's cradle." How does it work, and what does this device demonstrate about momentum and energy?

# WORDS TO UNDERSTAND

kinetic energy—the energy of movement.

mass—a measure of the amount of matter that makes up a substance or an object. Mass is given in grams. An object's mass remains the same wherever it is in the Universe.

momentum—a quality of a moving object, given by multiplying its mass by its velocity.

motion, laws of—three laws put forward by Isaac Newton to explain the behavior of moving objects. The laws state that:

(1) a moving body will continue to move in the same direction at the same speed unless something diverts it;

(2) any change in the speed or direction of a moving object depends on the size of the force acting on the object and the mass of the object; and

(3) for every action there is an equal and opposite reaction.

velocity—a measure of the speed and direction of travel of an object. In everyday life speed and velocity are usually used to mean the same thing.

vis viva—Literally "living force," a term introduced by Gottfried Leibniz to describe a quality of moving objects. It was similar to the later idea of kinetic energy.

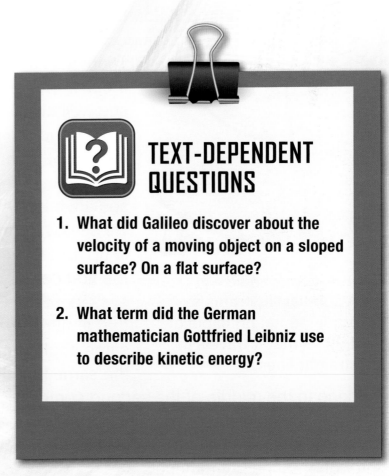

TEXT-DEPENDENT QUESTIONS

1. What did Galileo discover about the velocity of a moving object on a sloped surface? On a flat surface?

2. What term did the German mathematician Gottfried Leibniz use to describe kinetic energy?

Chapter 4

LETTING LIGHT

For many centuries people have tried to explain how we see and how light can produce shadows, reflections, rainbows and other colorful effects.

A sundial illustrates a fundamental principle of light — that it travels in straight lines.

The Greek philosopher Pythagoras (c.572–497 BCE) had the extraordinary idea that invisible rays come from the eyes and touch objects, and by doing so sense them. Sight, it was thought, was like a very delicate sense of touch. Democritus, who had put forward the notion of atoms, had another idea. He said that objects continually give off images of themselves that are picked up by the eyes.

There was an obvious drawback to these ideas. If either one of them was true, why couldn't you see well at night? Plato (427–347 BCE) tried to get around the problem by suggesting that an inner light, coming from the eyes, had to mix with the light from the Sun before we could see anything. Aristotle submitted the idea that we see by detecting rays from objects that are lit up, but this simple notion was rejected. In the first century CE, still using the rays from the eyes idea, the Greek engineer Hero showed that a mirror reflects back a beam of light at the same angle that it strikes the mirror. At about the same time Ptolemy, a Greek astronomer working in the middle of the second century CE, was also studying light. He showed how you can affect light in two ways: **reflection**, when it bounces off something, such as a mirror, and **refraction**, when the light bends as it passes through transparent materials.

WAVES OR PARTICLES?

The Greeks had two opposing views as to the nature of light itself, wherever they believed it came from. The first was that light is a disturbance in some invisible, undetectable substance that fills space. They called this substance **ether**, an idea that, yet again, was introduced by Aristotle. He saw light as being like a wave travelling through the ether just as a wave travels through water.

The other viewpoint was that light is a stream of tiny particles, too small and fast-moving to be seen individually. Plato and Aristotle both opposed this idea and for the next two thousand years or so it was more or less accepted that light was like a wave.

Roger Bacon carried out experiments to investigate how lenses worked.

Almost a thousand years later the Arab physicist Alhazen (965–1038) finally rejected the idea of beams of light from the eyes. He put forward the idea we accept today. Light from the Sun, a fire at night, or any other source of illumination, is reflected off the object and into the eyes. Alhazen studied lenses and mirrors and was interested both in the way light is reflected and how rainbows form.

The English scholar Robert Grosseteste (c.1168–1253) read Alhazen's works on light and carried out experiments of his own. He believed that the Universe was formed from light. Light was the first of all things to be created. It expanded from a point into a sphere and contained all other things within itself. This is startlingly similar to modern ideas of how the Universe formed, particularly if we think of light as a form of energy.

The English monk Roger Bacon (c.1214–1292) was a pupil of Grosseteste's and followed his teacher in studying light. Bacon is sometimes thought of as the first modern scientist. In sharp contrast to Aristotle, he put great emphasis on carrying out experiments. Some of his work involved the behavior of light and the way in which it can be bent and focused when it passes through a lens. He showed how a lens can be used as a magnifying glass and recommended spectacles for people with poor eyesight.

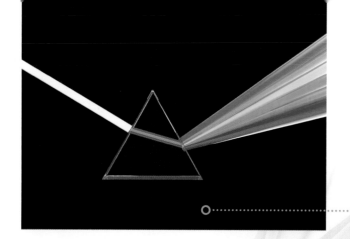

Newton showed that the spectrum produced by bending light through a prism consisted of the same colors visible in a rainbow. When light is refracted in this way some colors bend more than others. Violet light, for example, bends more than red light.

The next big step was taken by the astronomer Johannes Kepler (1571–1630). In 1610 Kepler borrowed one of the newly invented telescopes and began to find out just how it worked. Within six weeks he had proposed a theory that described how light and lenses behave, and how optical instruments could be designed by using his principles.

LIGHT OF MANY COLORS

Isaac Newton carried out a series of experiments with light and put forward some ideas as to what it is. He showed that you can split white light into a **spectrum** of different colors by passing light through a **prism**. He noted that light moves in straight lines and that the shadows it casts are sharp. To Newton it seemed obvious that light is a stream of particles moving from the object to the eyes and that it is not a wave. This is similar in some ways to the **quantum theory** that would be introduced by Max Planck 200 years later.

Isaac Newton used a prism to break white light into a spectrum of colors.

Thomas Young (1773–1829) was a man of such great intelligence that his fellow students at Cambridge University nicknamed him Phenomenon. He could read by the time he was two and read the Bible twice before he was four. He also learned to speak a dozen different languages, including Hebrew and Turkish.

Young tackled the problem of whether light comes in the form of waves or particles. As we have seen, Newton tended towards the view that particles are the answer. There had been a suggestion, however, that if the waves of light are very short then they would appear to travel in straight lines, like particles, and Young set out to see whether or not this is true.

In 1803 he carried out an experiment that was beautiful in its simplicity and effectiveness. First he made a small hole in a window blind. This hole was his source of light. Next he took a piece of card and made two pinholes in it, close together, and positioned it so that the sunlight coming through the hole in the window blind would pass through the pinholes and on to a screen behind them. What would you expect to happen? If the light was a stream of particles then there should be just two points of light on the screen where the particles went straight through the pinholes. On the other hand, if light was like a wave what would Young see?

Two years earlier, in 1801, Young had described an effect he called **interference**. If two or more waves meet they don't knock each other off course, but seem to pass straight through each other. You can see this if you watch raindrops hitting the surface of a pond. The ripples that spread out meet and cross each other and keep on going. What happens where the waves cross? The answer is that they combine, the peaks of one wave combining with the peaks of another to make a higher peak; if the trough of one wave meets the peak of another they cancel each other out.

Thomas Young carried out experiments to see whether light consists of waves or particles.

What Young saw on his screen between the two points of light from the pinholes was a series of curved, colored bands, the same shape as the ripples on the surface of a pond where two water waves meet. The dark areas between the bands were where the light waves cancelled each other out; the colored bands were where they added together. This seemed to be proof that light is like a wave.

Unfortunately Young's findings were not well received and he came in for some criticism for daring to contradict the great Newton! For the next 15 years it looked as though the **wave theory** would be forgotten and the **particle theory** would win. It was not until 1818 that the French physicist Augustin Fresnel (1788–1827) finally put an end to the particle theory. Then there was another problem. If light was like a wave, what was it travelling through? The next stage in understanding the nature of light came from the world of electricity.

WORDS TO UNDERSTAND

ether—an invisible, undetectable substance that was once thought to fill space.

interference—interference occurs when two or more waves pass through each other. Where the waves cross they add their energy together. If the crest of one wave coincides with the trough of another they cancel each other out. If two crests coincide they add to give a wave crest that is twice its big. Interference patterns show us where waves are adding and where they are cancelling. We can see this in the ripples caused by raindrops falling on the surface of a pond.

particle theory—the idea that light behaves as if it is a stream of particles.

prism—a block of glass or other transparent material that can be used to split white light into the visible spectrum.

quantum theory—the idea that energy comes in individual 'packets' called quanta (singular quantum).

reflection—the returning, or reflecting, of all or part of a stream of energy when it strikes a surface or the boundary between two different materials.

refraction—the change in direction of a stream of energy when it passes from one material into another.

spectrum—the name given to a range of different objects or properties arranged in order of magnitude. The spectrum of visible light ranges from red, which has the lowest energy, to violet, which has the highest energy.

wave theory—the idea that light behaves as if it is a wave.

TEXT-DEPENDENT QUESTIONS

1. What two opposing views did the Greeks hold about the nature of light?

2. What Arab physicist determined that light is reflected off objects and into the eyes?

3. How did Thomas Young show that light exhibited properties of a wave, rather than a particle?

RESEARCH PROJECT

Here's a simple experiment to show how rays of light can bend. For this experiment, take a plastic water bottle and poke a small hole in the side with a pencil, about one-third of the way from the bottom. Holding a finger over the hole, fill the bottle with water. Take an inexpensive laser pointer and line it up on the other side of the bottle so that it is shining on your finger covering the hole. Remove your finger and hold the pointer steady. The laser light should travel along the stream of water, bending down as it flows from the bottle. (Make sure you have a sink or container to catch the water!) This principle is similar to that used by fiber optic cables, which utilize light's properties to carry information.

Chapter 5

MAKING CONNECTIONS

The new electrical inventions of the nineteenth century helped scientists investigate whether electricity, light and magnetism are related forms of energy.

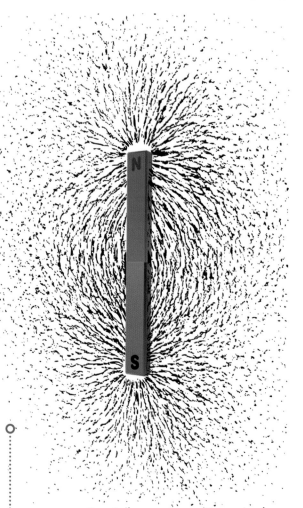

Iron filings can be used to show that a magnetic force field exists around a bar magnet. The concentration of filings at the poles of the magnet indicates that the field is strongest at those points.

By the middle of the nineteenth century electricity was well understood. More and more uses were being found for electrical energy. Electricity had transformed chemistry for one thing. Chemists could use this form of energy to split compounds that had resisted attempts to separate them out. Thanks to electricity many new elements had been discovered in this way including sodium and potassium by Sir Humphry Davy (1778–1829).

Scientists had succeeded in showing that electricity and magnetism were connected, almost like two sides of the same force. The Danish physicist Hans Christian Oersted (1777–1851) had recently shown that electricity can create a **magnetic field** and that a moving magnet is able to create an electric current. Using these findings Michael Faraday (1791–1867) had made the first electricity **generator**, in which the energy of a moving magnet was converted into electrical energy, and the first electric motor, which converted electrical energy into kinetic energy. Faraday suspected that there might be a connection between light, electricity, and magnetism, and in 1845 he discovered that he could affect a beam of light if he shone it between the poles of an **electromagnet**. He failed, however, to produce any effect when he used electricity alone.

FORCES AND FIELDS

To the end of his life Faraday believed that a link would be found. He had developed a new theory, called **field theory**, to explain the lines of force around a magnet. You can see the pattern of these lines of force if you scatter iron filings over a piece of paper covering a magnet. The filings form patterns around the magnet, which show where the

Michael Faraday worked out his field theory to explain the magnetic effects he observed.

lines of magnetic force are. Field theory said that the magnet was not the centre of a force, but rather an object that concentrated the lines of force through itself. The magnetic force wasn't in the magnet itself, but in the space that surrounded it, in the magnetic field. Faraday saw the lines of force as stretching out across ail of space and being concentrated around magnets, rather than the magnets themselves creating the fields.

Twenty years after Faraday developed field theory it was taken up by the Scottish physicist James Clerk Maxwell (1831–1879), who used it to show the relationship between light, electricity and magnetism that Faraday had searched for.

In 1865 Maxwell produced a set of four equations that brought together everything that was known about electricity and magnetism at that point. They described all the different aspects and behaviors of both forces. From his equations Maxwell proposed the existence of what he termed **electromagnetic waves**. He saw these as moving in an invisible field that combined both electrical and magnetic fields in a single phenomenon. He showed that the two were always bound together and that it was impossible to have electricity without magnetism and vice versa.

Faraday created this device, consisting of a coil of insulated wire held between the poles of a magnet, in 1831. He used it to show that magnetism could directly produce a spark of electricity, supporting his theory that electricity and magnetism were related.

You might try to imagine that an electromagnetic wave as being like two waves travelling in the same direction, but at right angles to one another. One of these waves is a magnetic field moving back and forth, or oscillating. The other is an electric field doing the same thing.

The two fields keep in step with each other as the electromagnetic wave travels along. Just as you can make waves in bathwater by moving your hand up and down, so an oscillating **electric charge** creates an electromagnetic wave.

By working out the ratios between certain electrical and magnetic effects, Maxwell was able to calculate the velocity of an electromagnetic wave. The answer came to around 300,000 kilometres per second. This was very close to the velocity that had been found by experiment for light. Maxwell, believing that this could not be a coincidence, had no hesitation in saying that light itself was a type of electromagnetic wave.

THE ELECTROMAGNETIC SPECTRUM

It seemed to Maxwell that there should be a whole range of electromagnetic waves or **radiations**, of which light was only a part. Invisible **infrared** and **ultraviolet** light had been discovered at either end of the visible spectrum and scientists had shown that these have the same properties as visible light. Maxwell predicted that more waves would be found beyond even these. After his death he was proved right with the discovery of **radio waves** and **X-rays**, which are both forms of electromagnetic radiation.

Maxwell is considered to be one of the geniuses of science, whose work ranks with that of Isaac Newton and Albert Einstein. His equations have stood the test of time. When Einstein upset everyone's ideas about the way the Universe works, Maxwell's equations stood up to the challenge and came through unaltered.

The discoveries of James Clerk Maxwell helped to launch the modern era of physics.

ELECTROMAGNETIC WAVES

An electromagnetic wave consists of two waves, an electric wave and a magnetic wave, moving at right angles to each other.

Radio transmissions have wavelengths of between 300 m and 1500 m. Televisions use radio waves with a wavelength of 0.5 m.

The microwaves used inside a microwave oven have wavelengths of between 10 cm and 1 mm.

The infrared radiation emitted by your body has a wavelength of about 0.000,05 m.

Visible light is made up of all the colors of the visible spectrum. They have wavelengths of about 0.000,000,5 m.

Ultraviolet rays are produced naturally by the Sun, but they can be made artificially. Their wavelength is 0.000,000,01 m.

X-rays pass through all but the densest parts of the body, such as bone. X-rays have a wavelength of 0.000,000,000,01 m.

Gamma rays are high- energy rays produced in a nuclear explosion. Their wavelength is 0.000,000,000,000,1 m.

WORDS TO UNDERSTAND

electric charge—a property of objects that gives rise to electrical and magnetic phenomena. Charge may be either positive or negative. Like charges repel one another and opposite charges attract.

electromagnet—a magnet consisting of a soft iron core, around which a coil of insulated wire is wound. When an electric current is passed through the wire the core becomes magnetized.

electromagnetic wave—waves of electromagnetic radiation travelling through space. An electromagnetic wave consists of an electric field and a magnetic field travelling in the same direction, but at right angles to one another. Light is a form of electromagnetic wave.

field theory—a theory that tries to explain how objects that are not in direct contact can affect each other. The field is the region in which an object feels a force as the result of another object or objects. Examples are the magnetic and gravitational fields.

generator—a machine for producing electricity from kinetic energy.

infrared—a type of invisible electromagnetic radiation with a wavelength longer than that of visible red light. It was discovered in 1800 by William Herschel.

magnetic field—the field of force that exists around a magnet. See field theory.

radiation—energy that travels in the form of waves, such as light, radio and X-rays. Radiation may also mean a stream of high-energy atomic particles, such as electrons.

radio waves—a type electromagnetic radiation with a very long wavelength, ranging from about 0.039 inches (1 millimeter) to 62 miles (100 km).

ultraviolet—a type of invisible electromagnetic radiation with a wavelength shorter than that of visible violet light, and with a higher energy. Some insects, such as bees, are able to detect ultraviolet light.

X-rays—a type of electromagnetic radiation with a very short wavelength and high energy, X-rays can pass through many materials.

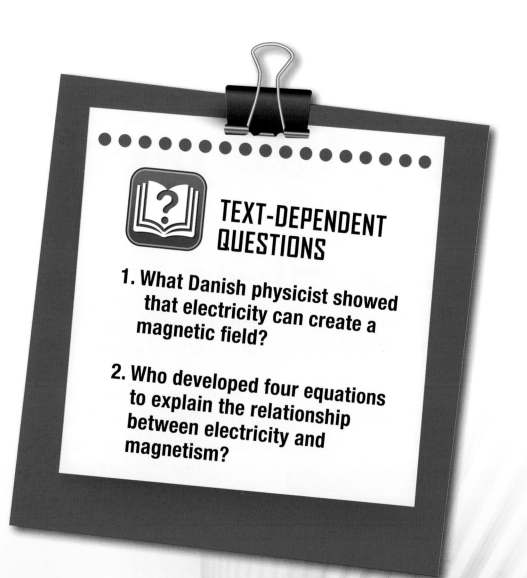

TEXT-DEPENDENT QUESTIONS

1. What Danish physicist showed that electricity can create a magnetic field?

2. Who developed four equations to explain the relationship between electricity and magnetism?

RESEARCH PROJECT

Here's a simple experiment to make an electromagnet. You will need a large (about 3 inches or 7.5 cm) iron nail, 3 feet (1 m) of thin coated copper wire, a D-sized battery, black electrical tape, and some paper clips (or other small metal items). To make the magnet, leave about 8 inches (20 cm) of wire loose at one end and wrap most of the rest of the wire around the nail. Try not to overlap the wires. Cut the wire if necessary, so that there is about another 8 inches (20 cm) loose at the other end. Remove about 1 inch (2.5 cm) of the plastic coating from both ends of the wire. Attach one end to the positive terminal of the battery, and the other end to the negative terminal with the electrical tape. When you point the nail near the paper clips or metal objects, the electricity from the battery charges the iron nail with a magnetic current, which should be strong enough to pick them up.

Chapter 6

LIQUID FIRE

Experiments carried out towards the end of the eighteenth century encouraged scientists to question the idea that heat is a sort of liquid.

During the seventeenth and eighteenth centuries scientists disagreed about the nature of heat. While some, including Galileo and Newton, argued that heat was a form of motion, most believed that heat is an invisible, weightless fluid. They claimed that everything flammable contains a mysterious substance called **phlogiston**, which is lost when a substance burns. The great French chemist Antoine Lavoisier (1743–1794) suggested that the heat fluid be called **caloric**. He believed that caloric flows from hot objects into cold ones. Lavoisier published a chemistry textbook in 1789 that included light and heat in its list of the chemical elements. He suggested that caloric surrounds the atoms of substances and when a chemical reaction takes place caloric is either added to or removed from the chemicals involved.

The French chemist Antoine Lavoisier explains the results of an experiment to his wife. Lavoisier believed that heat was an invisible liquid, which he called caloric.

CHALLENGE TO THE CALORIC THEORY

The caloric theory that heat is a fluid had been challenged by a Scottish chemist, Joseph Black (1728–1799). In a series of experiments he had shown that the same quantity of heat could cause different **temperature** rises, depending on the nature of the substance being heated. This couldn't be explained by thinking of a quantity of caloric fluid being poured into each substance.

The caloric view was further challenged by Count Rumford (1753–1814). Rumford was born Benjamin Thompson in Massachusetts, although he had fought on the British side in the American War of Independence. At the end of the war Rumford went to live in Europe. He entered the service of a German nobleman, the Elector of Bavaria, who gave him the title of count and made him Minister of War.

JOSEPH BLACK, M.D. F.R.S.E.
Late Professor of Chemistry in the University of Edinburgh.

Published March 31, 1800, by J. Hogg, N.42 Newman Street & J.P.Thompson, Great Newport Street, Long Acre.

Joseph Black's experiments helped to disprove the caloric theory.

As part of his duties he had to oversee the making of cannons for the Elector's army. A great deal of heat was generated when the drill bored out the barrels of the cannons and they had to be kept cool by throwing large amounts of water over them. The explanation that was given for this at the time was that the drill was releasing caloric trapped in the metal as it shaved off bits of it.

Count Rumford's observations of the heat produced when a cannon is bored out led him to believe that heat is a kind of motion.

Observing the heat produced by the drills led Rumford to reject the idea of caloric. As long as the drill kept working it could produce practically unlimited amounts of heat.

In fact, it could produce enough to melt the metal. How could the metal possibly have enough heat trapped inside to melt it? He also had a cannon drilled out under water and measured how long it took for the water to boil. He found that a given amount of water always took the same time to come to the boil. There never came a time when all the caloric had been removed from the cannon and no more heat appeared.

Rumford thought that there had to be a relationship between the work done by the drill and the amount of heat it produced, but he could not measure the heat precisely. He concluded that heat must be a form of motion. This was an important step forward in understanding energy. Heat was no longer something invisible and mysterious, but something that could be measured and experimented on by scientists. Rumford reported his findings to the Royal Society in London in 1798, but many physicists a rejected his findings and the caloric theory persisted for another 50 years.

WORDS TO UNDERSTAND

caloric—the name given by Antoine Lavoisier to the weightless fluid he believed was responsible for heat.

phlogiston—a substance, once thought to have been present in all flammable materials, that was released when they burned.

temperature—the property of an object that determines whether or not heat will flow to it from (or from it to) another object. Heat always moves from a region of high temperature to one of lower temperature.

RESEARCH PROJECT

Using your school library or the Internet, do some research on one of the following figures: Galileo Galilei, Isaac Newton, Humphry Davy, Hans Christian Oersted, Antonie Lavoisier, Joseph Black, Count Rumford, Michael Faraday, James Clerk Maxwell. Write a two-page report on this person's life and accomplishments, and share it with your class.

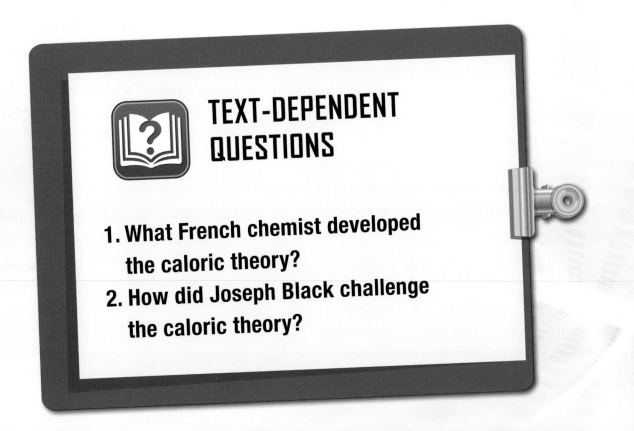

TEXT-DEPENDENT QUESTIONS

1. What French chemist developed the caloric theory?
2. How did Joseph Black challenge the caloric theory?

Chapter 7

STEAMING AHEAD

The development of steam power and the Industrial Revolution led many nineteenth-century scientists to look for ways to make the new machines even more effective.

Technology brought great improvements in steam engine design, particularly the engines designed by the Scottish engineer James Watt (1736–1819). What the steam engine basically does is to take heat from a heat source, its boiler, and change some of that heat into useful work. However, as much as 95 percent of the heat energy from the fuel burned in order to power the engine is wasted. Scientists thought that the only limit to the amount of work that could be done was in the quantity of fuel that could be burned to do it. Surprisingly, there was no scientific understanding of how the heat energy was converted into work by the steam engine. Knowing this would enable the engineers to build more efficient engines.

CARNOT'S PERFECT ENGINE

One of the first people to turn his mind to the problem was the French scientist Sadi Carnot (1796–1832). In 1824 he published *Reflections on the Motive Power of Fire*. It was the first book on the new science that came to be

The steam engine is a machine that converts the energy stored in a fuel, such as coal, into useful work. This might be used to pump water or to turn the wheels of a steam train. Hot steam at high pressure enters the cylinder and pushes the piston upwards. The piston raises a beam that then turns a flywheel and provides power. James Watt (opposite, top) improved early designs by adding a condenser and valves to keep the flywheel moving. His work led to advances in our understanding of heat energy.

called **thermodynamics**. This study of the connection between heat and work got its name from Greek words meaning "the movement of heat."

Carnot described how the perfect engine would behave and showed how its efficiency depends on heat flowing from a hot body to a cold one. In a steam engine heat goes from the boiler, where the steam is formed, to a cold chamber where the steam condenses back into water. The difference in temperature between the boiler and the cold chamber decides how well the engine works. It doesn't matter whether the temperature in between the two limits changes rapidly or slowly, or whether it goes down in stages or smoothly. Carnot's work showed that the 100 percent efficient engine is an impossible dream.

One person who played an important part in defining what we mean by energy was the English physicist James Prescott Joule (1818–1889). While helping to run his father's brewery Joule spent his spare time carrying out research. He was particularly interested in the new field of electrical power and in making better electric motors.

Michael Faraday had shown that the amount of electrical energy generated by a battery is closely related to the amount of metal used up while the battery is working. Joule then showed that the amount of heat generated by that electrical energy is the same as the heat produced if you burn an equal weight of the battery metal.

This is fine, but where is the combustion taking place when the electricity is being

CARNOT.

Sadi Carnot showed that the flow of heat energy between a hotter object and a cooler object depends on the difference in temperature between them.

James Joule, who worked out that one form of energy can be converted into the same amount of another form of energy.

produced using magnets in a generator? A series of experiments carried out between 1843 and 1847 led Joule to conclude that the heat is produced as a result of the mechanical motion of the moving parts of the generator. The *vis viva*, in other words. Joule measured both the work done to drive his generator and the amount of heat generated by the electric current it produced. He was able to show that a given amount of work always produced the same amount of heat. It didn't matter whether the mechanical energy was being used to compress air or stir a liquid, the heat produced was always the same.

In recognition of Joule's discovery that one form of energy can be converted into an equivalent amount of another form, a unit of energy, the **joule**, was named after him. One joule is about the amount of energy you would use to lift an apple a little more than three feet (1 meter) off the ground.

Joule's discovery formed the basis for what is known as the first law of thermodynamics. The idea that energy is conserved was first put forward by the German physicist Julius Mayer (1814–1878) in 1842, but his work did not receive much attention and the credit was given to Hermann Helmholtz (1821–1894), another German physicist. According to the first law, if you measure all the energy in an enclosed space (or **closed system** as physicists call it), before and after something happens you will find that the total amount of energy remains the same at the end as it was at the beginning. However, some of it will have changed from one form, say kinetic energy, into another, heat.

The German physicist Rudolf Clausius (1822–1888) showed that whenever work of any kind is done some of the energy is lost as heat, which cannot be recaptured and made to do useful work. Although Joule had shown that heat and work were equivalent the lost heat couldn't be converted back into work. Some of the steam engine's heat energy goes in warming up the air around it, for instance, rather than moving the piston.

ENTROPY AND THE DEATH OF THE UNIVERSE

The Irish-Scottish mathematician William Thomson (1824–1907), who later became Lord Kelvin, set out the second law of thermodynamics in 1851. According to this, mechanical work tends to turn into heat, but not the other way around. Everytime we do anything some of the energy we use is lost as heat.

In 1865 Rudolf Clausius introduced a concept he called **entropy**, from the Greek word meaning "change of form." He stated that entropy is always increasing and that it reaches its greatest extent whew there is no possibility of more work being done, all of the mechanical energy having been converted into heat.

Clausius was able to relate the laws of thermodynamics to the entire Universe. He did so by considering it as a closed system (after all, what could there be outside the Universe?). The first law, he said, states that the total energy of the Universe is constant. The second law states that the total entropy of the Universe is increasing all the time.

Hermann Helmholtz saw this as leading towards a Universe where one day all the energy would be spread out as heat, where there would be no further changes possible and all life would have vanished long before. This idea came to be known as the **heat death** of the Universe. Don't worry about it, however. If it does happen, it won't be for a very, very long time yet.

The standard unit used to measure energy is called a joule. The amount of energy it takes to lift an apple about 3.3 feet (1 m) off the ground is approximately one joule.

William Thomson, Lord Kelvin, did important research in the emerging field of thermodynamics.

WORDS TO UNDERSTAND

closed system—a physical system that is not in contact with anything outside itself. The Universe may be the ultimate closed system!

entropy—a measure of the disorder in a system and how the energy in that system is distributed among its atoms. When the energy is evenly distributed the system reaches its maximum entropy and no further changes can take place.

heat death—the idea that some time in the far distant future the Universe will reach a state of maximum entropy, when all of its energy will be evenly spread out and no further change will be possible.

joule—a unit of energy named after James Joule.

thermodynamics, laws of—thermodynamics is the study of the laws that determine the conversion of one form of energy into another, and of the ability of energy to do work. The first law of thermodynamics deals with the idea that energy cannot be created or destroyed, but changes from one form into another. The second law deals with the fact that heat cannot be transferred from a body of a lower temperature to one of a higher temperature, and that the entropy, or disorder, of a closed system will increase with time.

RESEARCH PROJECT

Here's a sweet way to demonstrate the second law of thermodynamics: make your own ice cream. When you add rock salt to ice, it lowers the temperature of the ice; this lower temperature is transferred to the warmer cream mixture, which chills it and creates the familiar ice-cream texture. Recipes for making homemade ice cream can be found online or in your school library.

TEXT-DEPENDENT QUESTIONS

1. Who wrote the first book on thermodynamics?

2. What did James Joule discover about energy?

3. Which German physicist is credited with the idea that energy is conserved?

Chapter 8

PACKETS OF ENERGY

During the early part of this century scientists developed a new theory to connect the different forms of energy in the Universe.

The years around the beginning of the twentieth century saw great changes in the way the whole idea of energy was approached. Max Planck (1858–1947), another German physicist, had been greatly influenced by the work of Clausius on thermodynamics and spent some years studying that subject before turning to the problem of something known as "the **ultraviolet catastrophe**."

If something is heated, a piece of metal say, it begins to glow, first dull and red, then orange, and then it becomes white hot and bright. If it is made even hotter it starts to give off ultraviolet rays. Also, if an object is completely black then it will absorb all the radiation that is directed at it and will reflect none of it. However, it will still lose heat by radiation as it gets hotter and hotter. This sort of radiation is called **black-body radiation** and black objects made from different materials will give off the same amount of black-body radiation at any particular temperature.

It was in describing black-body radiation that the great theory of the wave nature of light proposed by the Scottish scientist James Clerk Maxwell fell down. If it was true, different colors have different **frequencies**, or rates of vibration. As the temperature of an object rises it gives off light at higher and higher frequencies, moving up the spectrum from red to violet as the amount of energy it radiates increases.

Since a black object completely absorbs and radiates all frequencies of electromagnetic energy most of its radiation should be given off at high frequencies, in other words in the ultraviolet range and above. This is simply because there are more high frequencies than there are low ones. It means that the black body should give off a huge amount of radiation in one sudden ultraviolet flash. This didn't happen when scientists carried out experiments. The radiation given out by a black object is distributed unevenly across the spectrum, with a peak that depends on the black object's temperature.

Scientists tried to come up with equations that would explain why the black-body radiation behaves as it does. Although there were equations that explained how a black object radiates red light and equations that explained how light at the blue end of the spectrum is produced, there seemed to be no way of providing a complete explanation. That was the situation until Max Planck offered a solution that was radical and stunning. It was to transform physics.

THE QUANTUM UNIVERSE

In a speech given on 19 October 1900 at a meeting of the German Physical Society Planck announced a new age in physics. He suggested that energy exists in packets, or particles, like matter, rather than being regarded as something continuous that could be divided into smaller and smaller parts. He called these packets of energy *quanta* (singular **quantum**) from the Latin word meaning "how much?" Each quantum has its own frequency and **wavelength**. A quantum of violet light has twice the frequency and therefore twice the energy, of a quantum of red light.

The conclusion from this was that energy could only be emitted or absorbed in whole quanta. This meant that a black body was not

When you heat a black metal object, such as a poker, it starts to glow red. As you heat it more strongly, the poker emits yellow light. Finally, it becomes so hot that it radiates light at all wavelengths, which will make it appear white-hot.

likely, after all, to emit radiation equally across all of the wavelengths. It was much easier to give off a quantum of red light, as that required a relatively small amount of energy, than it was to give off a quantum of ultraviolet light, which required much more energy. The ultraviolet catastrophe didn't happen because, even though there were many, many more high frequencies, it required higher and higher energies to create quanta at those levels.

Objects go from red to orange to white as they heat up because the increasing amounts of heat energy available allow the higher energy quanta to be formed. What Planck had achieved was to show that energy and frequency were actually the same thing, just measured in different units. The relationship between frequency and energy came to be known as **Planck's constant**. The energy of a quantum of radiation can be calculated by multiplying its frequency by Planck's constant.

Planck himself thought that his explanation was unlikely because it contradicted everything he had been taught. Yet it worked, there could be no doubt, and he accepted it as a convenient explanation, but he tried for years to disprove it. The real consequences of his ideas, however, would be worked out by others.

Max Planck visualized energy as existing in tiny packets, or quanta. He said that there are different amounts of energy in the quanta found in each color (or wavelength) of light. For example, there is more energy in a blue quantum of light than in a red quantum. Scientists now call light quanta photons.

RESEARCH PROJECT

The U.S. Environmental Protection Agency has a website that explains radiation waves, available at http://www.epa.gov/radiation/understand/index.html.

black-body radiation—the electromagnetic radiation emitted by a body that absorbs all the radiation falling on it and as a result gets hotter and hotter.

frequency—the rate at which a regularly occurring event repeats itself. For example, the frequency of a wave tells you the number of times per second a wave crest will pass a particular point.

Planck's constant—a number that is equal to the ratio of the energy of a quantum to its frequency.

quantum—a packet of energy. The minimum amount by which the amount of energy in an object or a system can change. This idea, forms the basis of the quantum theory.

ultraviolet catastrophe—the belief that an object heated to a sufficient temperature would give off a huge quantity of radiation in a flash of ultraviolet light.

wavelength—the distance between one wavecrest and the next, or between two equivalent points on successive waves.

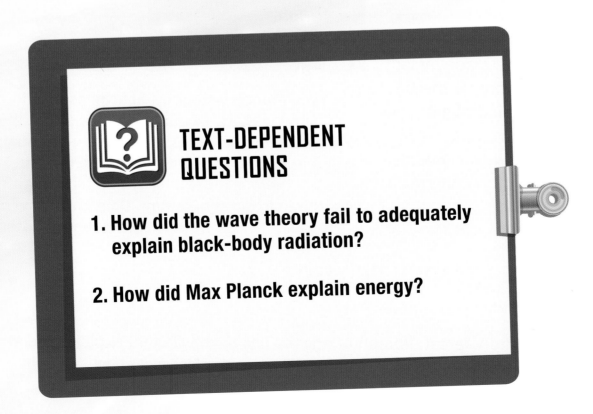

TEXT-DEPENDENT QUESTIONS

1. How did the wave theory fail to adequately explain black-body radiation?

2. How did Max Planck explain energy?

Chapter 9

ENTER EINSTEIN

The quantum theory of energy has led to further important discoveries that may help to satisfy the world's growing energy needs.

When Max Planck put forward his quantum theory Albert Einstein (1879–1955) was only 21. Five years later, while working as a clerk in the Patent Office in Berne, Switzerland, he produced three short scientific papers, each one of which pointed physics in a new direction. One of these papers succeeded in convincing scientists of the existence of atoms. The second paper we will come to shortly. The third was concerned with the phenomenon known as the **photoelectric effect**.

Scientists knew that when you shine light on a solid metal surface, **electrons**—tiny particles that are parts of atoms—are ejected from the metal. This is the photoelectric effect. The energy of these electrons depends only on the color, or frequency, of the light used, rather than on how bright it is. No matter how bright the light the electrons that emerge from the metal still have the same energy. This makes no sense if the old ideas about light are used. It seems obvious that the brighter the light the more energy it should have, but the photoelectric effect does not show this. Einstein realized that Planck had provided the answer. The beam of light should be thought of as being made up of tiny

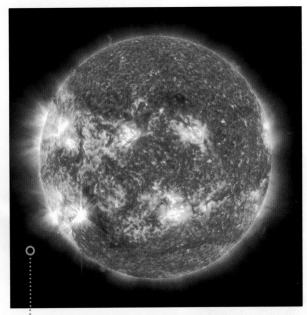

At very high temperatures the nuclei of small atoms can be made to join together to form larger ones. This is the process called nuclear fusion, which occurs constantly at the heart of stars, such as our Sun.

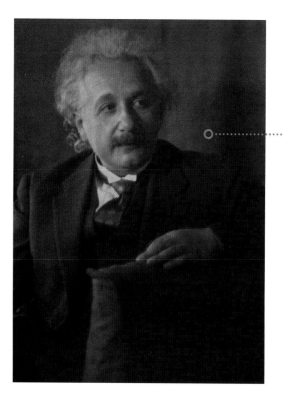

packets, which Einstein called "light quanta." When a light quantum strikes an electron the quantum's energy is transferred to the electron, which is shot out. The brighter the light the more quanta there are, so more electrons of the same energy will be ejected from the metal. The higher the frequency of the light the bigger are the quanta and the faster the electrons are ejected. Below a certain frequency the light quanta don't have enough energy to knock out any electrons.

Albert Einstein received the Nobel Prize for Physics in 1921 for his work on the photoelectric effect and quantum theory.

WAVES AND PARTICLES

As we have seen, Planck himself wasn't convinced that the quantum theory was true. Most physicists still believed that energy varies infinitely in its intensity and does not come in packets. They were reluctant to give up the idea that light behaves like a wave. After all, the wave idea gives clear explanations for the way light behaves in the everyday world, such as the way it is reflected and refracted and forms interference patterns.

The only way to establish whether or not Einstein was right was by experiment. By 1916 there was no longer any doubt, and by the 1920s scientists were having to completely rethink their ideas about light. Einstein had provided the proof that Max Planck was right. Yet Einstein, like Planck, had his doubts. Towards the end of his life he wrote in a letter to a friend that fifty years of pondering had not brought him any closer to answering the question "What are light quanta?"

What did become apparent was that both the wave and the particle (quantum) theories of light are correct. Depending on how you look at it, light is both a wave and a particle. The answer to the question "What is light?" is simply that light is light. There is nothing else we can compare it to. All we can do is describe how it behaves in different situations and, in order to do that, we have to assume that sometimes it behaves like a wave and sometimes it behaves like a stream of particles. What we are really doing is making mental models of the way light acts and we have no single model that will describe everything light does. Remember that models are all they are—we cannot hope to describe light as it really is. Do you remember, however, the problem we had a while back of what it was that light waves were passing through? Because light travels in little quantum packets, like particles, it doesn't have to travel through anything!

Richard Feynman contributed to the field of physics known as quantum electrodynamics, and won the 1965 Nobel Prize for his work.

There is, in fact, a theory that describes both the wave and particle properties of light. It is called **quantum electrodynamics**, or QED, and was first put forward in 1949 by Richard Feynman (1918–1988), Julian Schwinger (1918–1994), and Sin-Itiro Tomonaga (1906–1979), working independently. However QED involves complex mathematics and its ideas are even more difficult, if not impossible, to visualize, so we will not go into it here. Let us return to Einstein.

The second paper that Einstein published in 1905 really did change the way scientists and, eventually, just about everyone else, looked at the world. This was his special **theory of relativity**.

Among its many achievements it described the relationship between matter and energy. This is summarized in the famous equation, $E=mc^2$, in which E represents energy, m equals mass and c^2 is the velocity of light multiplied by itself. The velocity of light is a huge quantity so a small amount of mass is equivalent to a very large amount of energy.

This relationship explained, for example, that the some of the radiation given off by radioactive materials comes from an incredibly small amount of mass being converted into energy. The amounts involved were far too small to be measured in the chemistry laboratory but atomic scientists got to work on the problem and Einstein was soon proved right. By the 1950s, scientists had found a practical use for idea of converting mass into energy by developing nuclear power plants capable of generating electricity.

SOURCE OF THE SUN'S ENERGY

For a long time astronomers had puzzled over the possible source of the Sun's energy and that of all the other stars. Anaxagoras, whom we met at the beginning of the book, thought that the Sun was a large red-hot rock, about the size of mainland Greece! Later people had come up with more sophisticated ideas, but none fitted the facts. By the mid-twentieth century scientists knew that the Earth was about four-and-a-half billion years old, so the Sun had to have been burning for at least that long. Until Einstein published his ideas no known fuel could possibly last for that length of time. Special relativity had shown the answer. The fuel of the stars is atomic. Every second the Sun turns 5.1 million tons of its mass into energy, by the chain of reactions called **nuclear fusion**.

This is a staggering amount of energy, radiating out in all directions into space. Only a tiny amount of it reaches the Earth—less than a billionth part of the Sun's output, in fact—but this is enough to provide practically all the energy used on our planet. The Sun provides the heat that warms the planet and the light that illuminates it. Some of the sunlight is trapped by green plants and provides the energy for almost all life on the Earth. The Sun powers the Earth's weather systems. To put it into perspective, the solar energy that falls on the Earth every year is more than a thousand times the total amount of energy used annually by the entire human race. If scientists could find a controlled way to reproduce here on Earth the reactions that take place in the Sun, rather than unleashing them all at once in nuclear detonations, it would go a long way to meeting our ever-growing energy needs.

Wind-powered turbines and solar fields are utilized today to produce electrical power from renewable sources.

electron—one of the basic constituents of matter. Electrons carry a negative electric charge. All atoms are surrounded by a cloud of electrons.

nuclear fusion—a nuclear reaction in which smaller atoms fuse together to form larger atoms. In the process huge amounts of energy are released. The energy of stars is generated by nuclear fusion.

photoelectric effect—the release of electrons from a material exposed to electromagnetic radiation as a result of the transfer of energy from the photons of the electromagnetic radiation to the electrons in the material.

quantum electrodynamics—a theory put forward by Richard Feynman and others to explain how light (and other forms of electromagnetic radiation)can sometimes act as if it is a wave and sometimes as if it is a stream of particles.

theory of relativity—one of the great achievements of Albert Einstein. Among other things, the theory set out the relationship between matter and energy, showing them to be two sides of the same phenomenon.

TEXT-DEPENDENT QUESTIONS

1. What is the answer to the question, "What is light?"

2. What theory describes both the wave and particle properties of light?

RESEARCH PROJECT

A simple explanation of how nuclear power plants work is provided online at www.ucsusa. org/nuclear-power/nuclear-power-technology/how-nuclear-power-works#. VehrGSgcja4

SERIES GLOSSARY OF KEY TERMS

anomaly—something that differs from the expectations generated by an established scientific idea. Anomalous observations may inspire scientists to reconsider, modify, or come up with alternatives to an accepted theory or hypothesis.

evidence—test results and/or observations that may either help support or help refute a scientific idea. In general, raw data are considered evidence only once they have been interpreted in a way that reflects on the accuracy of a scientific idea. **experiment**—a scientific test that involves manipulating some factor or factors in a system in order to see how those changes affect the outcome or behavior of the system.

hypothesis—a proposed explanation for a fairly narrow set of phenomena, usually based on prior experience, scientific background knowledge, preliminary observations, and logic.

natural world—all the components of the physical universe, as well as the natural forces at work on those things.

objective—to consider and represent facts without being influenced by biases, opinions, or emotions. Scientists strive to be objective, not subjective, in their reasoning about scientific issues.

observe—to note, record, or attend to a result, occurrence, or phenomenon. **science**—knowledge of the natural world, as well as the process through which that knowledge is built through testing ideas with evidence gathered from the natural world.

subjective—referring to something that is influenced by biases, opinions, and/or emotions. Scientists strive to be objective, not subjective, in their reasoning about scientific issues.

test—an observation or experiment that could provide evidence regarding the accuracy of a scientific idea. Testing involves figuring out what one would expect to observe if an idea were correct and comparing that expectation to what one actually observes.

theory—a broad, natural explanation for a wide range of phenomena in science. Theories are concise, coherent, systematic, predictive, and broadly applicable, often integrating and generalizing many hypotheses. Theories accepted by the scientific community are generally strongly supported by many different lines of evidence. However, theories may be modified or overturned as new evidence is discovered.

FURTHER READING

Andrews, John, and Nick Jelley. *Energy Science: Principles, Technologies, and Impacts.* New York: Oxford University Press, 2013.

Churchill, Richard, et al. *365 Simple Science Experiments with Everyday Materials.* New York: Sterling Publishing Company, 2013.

Forbes, Nancy, and Basil Mahon. *Faraday, Maxwell, and the Electromagnetic Field: How Two Men Revolutionized Physics.* Amherst, N.Y.: Prometheus Books, 2014.

Heilbron, John L. *Galileo.* New York: Oxford University Press, 2012.

LeVine, Harry. *The Great Explainer: The Story of Richard Feynman.* Greensboro, N.C.: Morgan Reynolds, 2009.

Pohlen, Jerome. *Einstein and Relativity for Kids.* Chicago: Chicago Review Press, 2012.

The Science Book: Everything You Need to Know about the World and How It Works. Washington, D.C.: National Geographic, 2011.

INTERNET RESOURCES

http://www.physics4kids.com
The website Physics for Kids has a great deal of information on energy, motion, electricity, magnetism, and thermodynamics, provided in a way that is easy for young people to understand.

http://www.fnal.gov/pub/science/inquiring/matter
This article on the science of matter, space, and time, with links to additional material, is provided by Fermilab, the premier U.S. particle physics laboratory, which is exploring the smallest building blocks of the matter that makes up the universe.

http://www.pbs.org/wgbh/nova/blogs/physics/2015/02/brief-history-speed-light
This web page from the PBS program NOVA provides information about the speed of light.

http://www.biology4kids.com/files/studies_scimethod.html
A simple explanation of the scientific method is available at this website for young people.

http://www.livescience.com
The website Live Science is regularly updated with articles on scientific topics and new developments or discoveries.

https://kids.usa.gov/science/index.shtml
This U.S. government portal includes links to projects and science experiments for young people.

INDEX

Numbers in **bold italics** refer to captions.